somewhere
in advance
of
nowhere

Jayne Cortez

somewhere in advance of *nowhere*

NEW YORK / LONDON

Library of Congress Catalog Card Number: 95–72973

Copyright © 1996 by Jayne Cortez

The right of Jayne Cortez to be identified as the author
of this work has been asserted by her in accordance with the Copyright, Designs
and Patents Act 1988

All rights reserved under the International and
Pan-American Copyright Conventions

First published in 1996 by Serpent's Tail,
4 Blackstock Mews, London N4, and
180 Varick Street, 10th Floor, New York, NY 10014

Drawings by Melvin Edwards

Cover design by Rex Ray
Phototypeset by Intype London Ltd
Printed in Finland by Werner Söderström Oy

Contents

About Flyin' Home	1
Visita	3
Adupe	7
In 1985 I Met Nicolás Guillén	11
In Gilberto de la Nuez's Studio	12
Woman On Burro In Asilah	13
Do Not Allow	15
Arizona 1985	16
Shut Off the System	19
Another Tropical Night	20
What Do You Think (Centennial 86)	21
You Have	23
Poetry	24
Samba Is Power	26
The Man with Elephantiasis Leg in Recife Brazil	29
New York's Bullfighter Gums	32
The Summit	33
These New York City Pigeons	34
1988 Now What	37
Super Poets of Guadalajara	39
Poet Cover Your Feet	41
Neighbor	43
The Dreams	44
Dear Banjo	47
Don't Ask 1980	48
Atmospheric Burn	51
I Have Been Searching	53
To Chrysler Cirrus	55
I Wonder Who	56
The Guitars I Used To Know	59

What Can We Sing for You	63
The Arrival	64
I Got the Blue-Ooze 93	65
Whatever Frightens	67
Why Not (Babs Gonzales)	68
The Oppressionists	71
I'm Gonna	72
A Miles Davis Trumpet	73
So What	77
The Harmattan	79
There Are No Stars	80
Bumblebee, You Saw Big Mama	81
Me	84
Global Inequalities	85
Compañera (Ana Mendieta)	87
Be Good Enough	90
At a Certain Moment in History	92
Now I Dig Up Patinas	94
She Got He Got	96
The Heavy Headed Dance	100
The Gulf Tones	103
Say It	104
Don't Write	107
Sacred Trees	109
States of Motion	113
Find Your Own Voice	116
Glossary	119

Special Thanks to Melvin Edwards and Bob Rogers

About Flyin' Home

What would you say to yourself
if you had to lay on your back
hold up the horn
& play 99 courses of
a tune called Flyin' Home
exactly as you recorded it
55 years ago
& what would you think
if you woke up in the afternoon
& your head was still spinning with
voices shouting
Flyin' Home blow Flyin' Home
& what would you do
if someone whispered in your ear
hug me kiss me anything
but please don't play Flyin' Home
& what if a customer said:
tonight I'm having sex with
a person who has been up
in a flying saucer
so please funk me down good with Flyin' Home
& what would you think
if someone started singing
Yankee Doodle Dandy
in the middle of your solo on Flyin' Home
& what if you had to enter
all the contaminated areas in the world
just to perform your infectious version of
Flyin' Home
& what if you saw yourself

looking like a madman
with a smashed horn
walking backward on a subway platform
after 50 years of blowing Flyin' Home
& what would you think to yourself
if you had to play Flyin' Home
when you didn't have
a home to fly to
& what if Flyin' Home became
your boogie woogie social security check
your oldie but goodie way out of retirement
& was more valuable than you
I mean somewhere
in advance of nowhere
you are in here
after being out there
Flyin' Home

Visita

1981
in Cuba
looking for
the great poet
Nicolás Guillén
in La Habana
in El Vedado
& on street corners
with 'Johnny Ordinary'
in bars with
'Johnny Nobody' &
between receptions & presentations
at Union of Artists & Writers
in office of Vice Minister of Culture
in the forest of ruffled tail feathers
at Tropicana night club
& in Santiago
Santiago de Cuba
where Jose Marti is buried like
        a perfect poem
where spirit of Antonio Maceo sits like
        a bronze sunrise
where beauty of Mariana Grajales who
saw her fifteen sons fall into
claws of fifteen buzzards
        circulates
where blood of heroes illuminate in
deepness of Moncada barracks
where old trova come leaping from new trova
& we are the trovas on the road to Bayamo

the road where I swear I hear
bass droning voice of Jesuś Menendez
I swear I see those black facial gestures
meeting my facial gestures
in brightness of the cane field that
spins before me like a dream of
the sun dressed in fuchsia and
melting into folk lyrics of Camaquey
& merging with lime colored palm leaves
& blowing with tobacco smoke through
X cross section of
everything cross & criss-crossing like bulls
flywings   goats   dry grass   horses   gauchos
& this bus this guagua pulling
into city of huge clay pots
city of clear water
city of charcoal reddish mud
city of caramel sand
city with Indian name Camaquey
Camaquey City
birthplace of Nicolás Guillén
special like the clay pots
caramel like the sand &
in advance of walking on
        Trinidad cobblestones
& before passing Sani Spiritus
        Sierra del Escambray
then returning to
        La Habana
for homage
to Wilfredo Lam
it would be so nice
to meet Nicolás Guillén

here at the friendship house
or in a study circle
or with the Federation of Women
it would be so nice
to meet the poet who
gave us the Riddles
the Tropics
the Great Zoo
& Che Commandante
I would like to meet Nicolás Guillén
before leaving the
1952 turquoise Studebaker
the 1948 red painted Dynaflow Buick
the 1955 lemon yellow Chevy
& the steamrolling
diesel truck in the sky
honk   honk   honk
I would like to meet Nicolás Guillén while
I'm dazzling in the pure energy of Cuba
& getting the same serene feeling I get
after arriving in West Africa
no heavy load of racism on my shoulders
& while I feel happy
about nothing in particular
just happy
like a baby in the baby brigade
like children in child care centers
not fearful of knowing each other
just free & jaunty
you know jauntiness
not in the dumps of
constant depression
not hanging on edge

of an epidemic of stress
but cheerful & sunny
like sun bursting through pollution
on late stormy afternoons understand
not soft not hard core not threatened
but protected
& I would like to
meet Nicolás Guillén
in this mood
in this place
at this time

Aduepe
(ah doo pway)

1981
& I did not find Nicolás Guillén
but I found Cuba
the Cuba in Nicolás Guillén's poetry
poetry dedicated
to his two selves
his two sides
poetry in half notes
in eighth notes
in 6/8 time
poetry moving backward & forward
like war dances
poetry doing the Rara
in an African vocabulary
poetry of Nicolás Guillén
Nicolás Banjo Guitar Mbira Guillén
improvising like
the great instrument he is
in Yoruba
in Spanish
in Son
not exotic but Zydeco
Not Miami but Havana
not tweet tweet but Mau Mau
Adupe to the man
from Camaquey

This morning I went
into the Paris

of his poetry
& came out with poets
clinking glasses to
Nouveau Beaujolais at Roquets
I pushed into
Favela of his poetry
and emerged with
carnival costumes
for one hundred year
celebration of the
abolition of slavery
I looked through
his blunt poetry
& saw exiles smiling
like rusty bulldozers
& acting like disjointed
chiefs of staff
like broken stags roaming
in everglades of khaki teeth
& clandestine scrotum
I walked through
seance house of his poetry
& came upon fiesta sizzling
in bubble chamber of Aztec clouds
I dived into political content of his poetry
and discovered mysterious caves with
odors of rotting imperialist dust
I looked at shell-lined pelvis of his poetry
and saw infra-green heat of human capacity
snaking down through underground galaxy
of atomic clocks
I moved into
stamina of his poetry & returned

with boxing gloves smelling like
Santeria shrines
I ran along the Malecon of his poetry
& found a poverty imbued
with the power to drive straight through
a northern frente frio
I stood in stadium of his staccato
yelping poetry and heard messages coded
& covered with drum heads from Oyo
and I said Adupe Nicolás Guillén
Adupe
for the cavalcade of leaves &
moaning doves & regalia of punching bags
Adupe
for the musky cyclones in bolero Jackets
& smoke filled consultation of yagruma trees
Adupe
for the call & response of collaborating oceans
& the rooster juice splashed on feet
steeped in rumba motivations
Adupe
for the great poem confrontations
of Nicolás Guillén
Adupe
determination belongs to Guillén
revolutionary thought belongs to Guillén
solidarity belongs to Guillén
Gulla   Efik   Ewe   Fula   Fulani   Twi
belongs to Guillén
Mende   Mandingo   Mossi   Umbundu   Suk
belongs to Guillén
Bomba La conga bomba
belongs to Guillén

Negrismo   Socialismo   belongs to Guillén
completeness of life in poetry
belongs to Guillén

Nicolas   Banjo   Guitar   Mbira   Guillén
digging up roots & making his mark
making his mark
breaking those chains & making his mark
making his mark
mixing up rhythms & making his mark
making his mark
talking to his people & making his mark
making his mark
working with his work & making his mark
making his mark
Nicolas   Banjo   Guitar   Mbira   Guillén
Nicolas   Banjo   Guitar   Mbira   Guillén
making his mark

In 1985 I Met Nicolás Guillén

In 1985 I met Nicolás Guillén while
he sat with admirers in Havana
I met Nicolás Guillén
as he listened to
school children sing his poems
I met Nicolás Guillén
introduced by Nancy Morejón
to the delegation of
African American women writers
I met Nicolás Guillén
while he joked & flirted
& made poetry out of
simple human kinds of things
I met Nicolás Guillén
with his wit
with his smile
with his social criticism
& Spanish all fast
& dished up spicy

In Gilberto de la Nuez's Studio

I am full of Gilberto's paintings
full of his forests & figures of
emancipated African ancestors
full of his conga drums, dancing lines
& human songbirds singing in the plaza with
rumba bands playing 'Yolanda Yolanda'

It's a warm November morning in El Vedado
Gilberto has lost weight
his hands are shaking
he confesses his circulation is poor
and going to the doctor is complicated
due to lack of petrol and
shortages of medical supplies

I think goddam this stupid
U.S. blockade of Cuba because
Cuba wants to be Cuban

It's a warm November morning
I can hear Gilberto saying:
It's 1991 and I don't have
      enough electricity
I don't have enough food
I don't have enough of enough
but I'm still a revolutionary
in control of my own thoughts
I'm still a painter
in control of these brushes
and even though my health is bad
I still support the Cuban Revolution

Woman On Burro In Asilah

Your burro
is not
just some
happy-go-lucky model
in a fashion show
your burro is a mechanic
a gospel recording artist
with two tambourine ears
& a psychic who knows when you need
another pair of buttocks to exist in
another set of lips to whistle through
another group of fingers to shout between
your burro pounds the ground and sees
not only solitude is great
you sit on that burro
& in walks the environment
out step the confessions
& it's one fine laxative night
one more lovely field of lava
your burro pulling & plowing &
pushing forward like a space ship & grinning
& carrying you like a rainbow carries water
up the dirt path
down the paved road
around the planet
& back
to swallow the sunset
then start again
from exact spot
where I say to you

if my pen put in
same mileage a day
as your burro
without dropping dead from
exhaustion
I would show my appreciation
by celebrating
the next two centuries right now
& what a fucking wonderful event

Do Not Allow

Do not allow flies to dominate your day
or let mosquitoes control your night
you are five slaps away from paradise
bring back the brown omelette
the green melon
& make that pony pull your wagon through
triangular sun sinking into
revolving earth
at the tone of trains whistling in from Tangier
at the sight of calamares frying between teeth
at the sound of your heart alive & thumping on
the water bottles of Asilah

Arizona 1985

Arizona
I have come
to sip
from your
coyote lips
I have come
to drink
from your
old Indian ears
and nothing else matters
because already
Afrikaaner bosses
have shit on their shoes
in Pretoria
A gigantic female typhoon brews
in the Pacific
sparks are blowing
from fat face of Baby Doc in Haiti
& I am here
but I don't see
profile of Geronimo
carved in the mountain
I don't smell
black shake dancer's sweat
on this gravel
& where are those
spider women from Naco

Arizona
I had to fly
over smoking skies of Philadelphia
swim through stagnant waters of
breeding mosquitoes in New Jersey
walk through stinging sandstorms in Morocco
sit on the airplane
next to groups of
ku klux klanish speaking tourists
to get here
So I'm not in the mood
      to quiver and grow numb
          with cockfighters
or get high &
sing along with
      mariachi bands
I'm not interested in
scribbling a few lines about
transnational solitude
   of your lavender pit
or concerned about penetrating
     your secret river of
      copper vomit and
    right-wing bird droppings

Arizona
re-introduce me
to the cliff dwellers
the water clan
the ghosts
in prehistoric caves
unfasten your cactus
your ore
your petrified forest
& give me
the Papago words of Papago
the Apache look of Apache
the Hopi view of Hopi
the Navaho dialogue with Navaho
Arizona
open up your silver slab of teeth

Shut Off the System

They're pulling
human pieces of flesh
from nervous rectum
of a Black Philly Flame of Hope
sue the city
the county
the state of bourgeois fear
don't give us
the classical story
of classical excuses
from
Mister Classical
drop-the-bomb-on-the-house-Goode
no good
cancel the classes
slash the certificates
seal up roof top to the planet

Another Tropical Night

Another tropical night
in house of a poet of tropical nights

Draw back the sweat
the slurs the eyes
& tell me what I'm missing
me I won't touch it

Here in presence of everything smacking
I see the same mouth of spittle
on lisp of same old prayer
same gestures shoving cotton balls
up ass of same old muck
same nobody undulating with
the same old shadow of guts

And above moisture of hands
& tangle of tongues
no way out

Go ahead
ask me about the plastic flowers
break a melodrama in front of my face

Again song of violent clicks
in throat of poet of tropical nights &
are there nicknames for such inverted moments
such hyperactive jumping beans turning the other cheek

Be still sweet syllable shits
because tonight I'm going to swallow
earwax of every cult in this hole

What Do You Think
(Centennial 86)

What do you think
what are your thoughts

Should we halt this ceremony
in the chocolate green river
stop opportunity from
spinning its helicopter blades
shove bar-b-que ribs through
Ms. Liberty's nose
carry that platform off in
a blimp of orange leather lips
on this birthday celebration weekend of
bugles   warships   jerked beef
rubber diadems
& the feathery mouth of Lady Chipmunk

What do you think
what are your thoughts

Should we step into
iron shell of the statue
& salute the sculptor's vision
before another woman opens
her sandwich of vegetarian lizards
Should we sit
in front of orchestra B
& watch two presidents knock
tooth picks together in a hunger for dead trees
or return to our seats after

incense smoke blows from
combat boots of
sheet wearing vendors

What do you think

Should we fill the exaggerated bronze coiffure
with French wine
to keep grand colossal mademoiselle Liberty
drunk & waving bonjour
in the New York harbor forever

What are your thoughts
on this birthday celebration weekend
of brass bands hairy nostrils
& eagle face friendship grins

You Have

You have
so much oomph
so much gaucho itch
so much unchecked violence of
        genitalia laugh
but do you have
a pass
  to start
    this affair
can you provide
urine samples
tattoo needles
one five minute high
a little inflammation on
        the heart muscle
a little parental guidance
        in the retina
a little salvation
    for the secreta

Poetry

In fact
poetry
will not
strike
lightning
through
any
convoy of chickens

Today poems are like flags
flying on liquor store roof
poems are like baboons
waiting to be fed by tourists

& does it matter
how many metaphors
reach out to you
when the sun
goes down like
a stuffed bird in
tropical forest
of your solitude

In fact
poetry
will not
sing jazz
through
constricted mouth
of an anteater

no matter how many
symbols survive
to see the moon
dying in saw dust
of your toenail

Samba is Power

In Brazil
I sambaed on the road to Joa Pesoa
I sambaed on the beach of transparent crabs
I sambaed to sounds of iron bells
in State of Bahia
I sambaed while eating muqueca
while watching capoiera
while wearing Oxum belt made by
maker of ritual objects in Salvador
I sambaed through São Paulo airport
sambaed into dark-skin   light-skin   African
Indian   Portuguese situations of struggle
I sambaed into translations while drinking batidas
with writers at Eboni Bookstore
I sambaed while waiting for a short mustached
so-called mulatto who swore
he was a Yoruba Babalawo   I sambaed
I sambaed onto corner of handcuffed
Afro-Brazilian men
sambaed next to women who were
spinning pulsating & assaulting police cars
I sambaed into house of condomble
into congress of Black culture
Into Perfil of African Literature
I sambaed
I sambaed next to the red buildings of Exu
I sambaed with Ge Ge & Egbas
I sambaed into trance of Yemaya
I sambaed with Oko
I sambaed in front of the daughters of Santos

I sambaed against walls of political grafitti
I sambaed with Shango
I sambaed with Mai do Samba
My samba wrapped in orisha ribbons
my samba mixed with human smells & feijoada
my samba infused with vatapa & caprinhas
the up hill samba bursting out of my feet
the samba whistles hollering out of my navel
the samba fetishes buzzing high
in sambadome of my soul
as I sambaed & sambaed & sambaed & sambaed
I sambaed diagonally through Recife floods
sambaed upward through steel cages of Brasilia
sambaed away from alcohol fumes
in Copacabana
sambaed behind homeless children
with soccer ball eyes
sambaed past dealers dealing drugs
sambaed into costume room
in communedado Mangueira
sambaed in front of protestant missionaries
who preached that samba is sin
but samba is life
samba is friction
samba is power
& I sambaed & sambaed & sambaed
sambaed into circles with Rei Mo Mo
as he shook his heavy flesh in slow motion
sambaed next to young women quivering
their brown calves in quadruple time
my samba getting drunk off the high speed rhythms
my samba embedded with bass drums of cachca
my samba parading & scorching teeth of

the Rio de Janeiro sun
my samba absorbing the forest stench
of poet from Amazonas
my samba squatting down & wiggling up
as I sambaed the samba of my memory
the samba of my fantasy
the samba of my samba
because samba is life
samba is friction
samba is power
samba is everything
that's why I sambaed & sambaed & sambaed

The Man with Elephantiasis Leg in Recife Brazil

This leg
oh yes
this leg he said
this leg is
a good luck charm
a torpedo of fission
a hissing chain that
lays itself down to sleep across
entrances to city markets
oh yes
This leg is
a lipstick-wearing dancer in samba schools
a fat snake that zigzags and
sells poetry pamphlets to strangers before
stall keepers open teeth to yell 'guarana'
oh yes
This leg is more than
colonized chapel of parasites
more than any tree of
slashed flesh & calcified sap
This leg is not
just a man-made dam of
filarial worms & feathers erupting through
winter smells of leather
This leg is
the legendary limb that has
an ancient grandfather who
stands in a plaque
on wall of the British Museum
and a twin sister who

leans against buildings in Chicago
and one cousin who
sits in the shade next to
certain hotels in Egypt
oh yes
this leg
This leg is
a tropical garden
a gas pump
a mountain of sea-foaming blood that
sleeps after midnight
has no football in hell
no bicycle in heaven
but rises like
sweet sausage tongue of the sun
to spit out poems before
the rootmen scrape their barks to holler 'guarana'
oh yes
This leg
oh yes

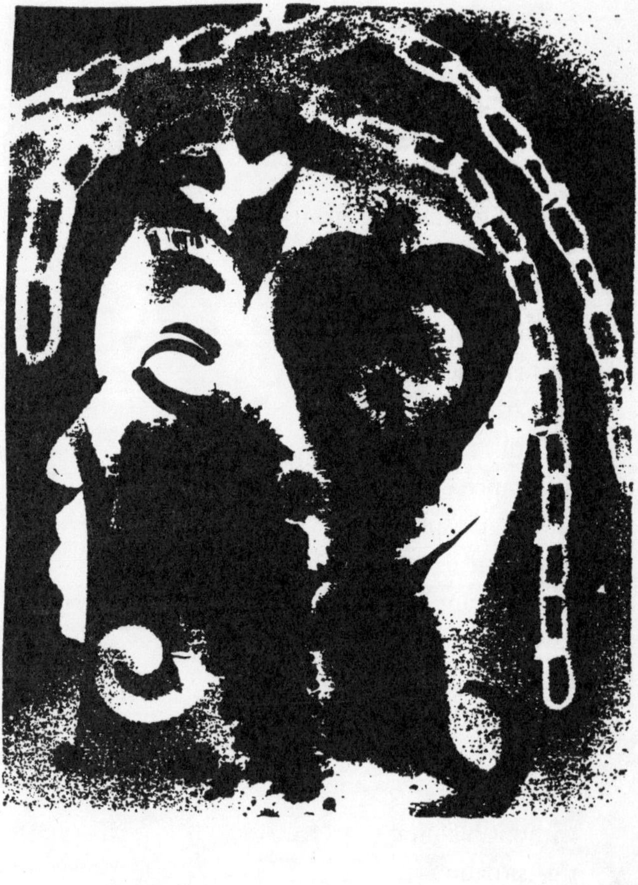

New York's Bullfighter Gums

New York's bullfighter gums
mashed up like red bananas
fiery sauce caked on
its rocket-shaped head
E train eyes rolling like
some big time frog from Uruguay
& I say
it's not impossible
to find deep fried romance
in this concrete ocean
of marinated snake juice
It's not impossible
to balance out life
in heated asphalt of
this suicidal lip track
let novocain & fortune cookies
have a recess in zero
because without naming
another name
without pointing
another finger
without blaming
this situation
on that contradiction
here's to friendship
dialogue   dreams
& the diplomatic pouch

The Summit

A meeting
between two men
two views
two arms devoted to racing
two old landfills dumped
in office of boozing eagles
in bureau of carousing penguins
vodka of my hiccuping pencil
scotch of my vomiting eraser
and everything depends
on this day's drunken storm of prayer
this day's ice-breaking calm
at the bottom of the summit
of polyester pants
tonight in cloudy eyes of irritated marines
tomorrow in dead spot of the index

These New York City Pigeons

These New York City Pigeons
cooing in the air shaft
are responsible for me
stumping my toe
spraining my ankle
& getting sick on ammonia fumes

That pigeon roosting on the clothes line
stole my nightgown
Those pigeons on the street lamp
made me feel foolish
while riding in a black car
completely splattered
with their grey & white poo poo

These New York City pigeons
are not calm like pigeons of Oxala in Brazil
and do not croon like doves of Zimbabwe

New York City pigeons moan
strange   low   mournful   quivering cancer like moans
mixed with
hungry hyena barks
& gulping loss of the forest cries

New York City pigeons
are not relaxed like
pigeons sunning at
Marcel Duchamp swimming pool in San Francisco

New York City pigeons
flap viral feather fungus dust from wings into faces
then sit on steps vocalizing & waiting
for the death of humankind

New York City pigeons
are not friendly like
pigeons eating flaky crescent-shaped rolls at
Hotel Du Piemont in Paris

New York City pigeons
are not content
like pigeons
posing for photos on arms
of men in plaza of Caracas

New York City pigeons
will lounge on ledges
& murmur profanity all day
will fight for fucking space in
the mating season
shit on air conditioners
& wipe their asses on windows
while big cockroaches
suck sucrets in the dark

New York City pigeons
are not alert
like pigeons
sitting quietly on bicycles
in peace memorial park of Hiroshima

New York City pigeons

roll their pearly eyes
inflate their throats
& defecate on the shoulders of pedestrians

New York City pigeons
have no love for crumb-throwing pigeon lovers
& no year of the pigeon is celebrated
at least
not for these New York City Pigeons

1988 Now What

So we get high
           pick teeth
                      wiggle tongues
                                    now what
I gave up
    my blue cross
        blue shield
            certificate
                of health
When
    one
        of
                    the most active
                    urine drinkers
                    in the west
                    became president
                                now what
dehorn a rhino
            so somebody's dick
                        can get hard
Burn the planet up
                in space
                      so somebody
                            can have
                                  an orgasm

```
brilliant
    great
        toxic waste
                    now what
                (my ass blew up last night
                my breath stinks
                & I'm here trying
                        to make the best of it)
                    now what
Are we
    out of control
        Is this extinction time
                            me
                                you
                                    and
                                        the elephant
                                                now
                                                    what
                                                what
                                            now
```

Super Poets of Guadalajara

Before you puff up
& become a flying peacock
surrounded by singing chickens
hear this
in Guadalajara
the super strong passionate
intensification poet is still
painter Jose Clemente Orozco
> The adult marimba players
> saying what they think marimbas
> should say
> if marimbas could talk
> behave like
> super humorous poets

Women holding audiences spell-bound
with their medicinal predictions while
pounding tortillas in Tonala Market
are called
super fascinating tone poets
> The men harmonically blending voices
> & splitting melancholy notes
> for video cameras every
> night in Mariachi Plaza
> are known as
> super sensitive poets with guts

Children who leave
tiny tin hearts on tourists' tables
transform themselves daily into
super professional beggar poets
> The politicians

   selling pieces of
   Mexico on
   the global market
   are not known as
   super poets
   but super greedy bandits
& it is not
poetry on the page that's hot
but poems written in stone by
super active avant garde poets.
Pancho Villa Vargos Rosita Morales
Little Indio Nogalas & Mestiza Lopez
working at the cement factory and
having conversations with
Señora unfinished revolution

Poet Cover Your Feet

It's raining excessively
on the Chelsea Hotel canopy
on hood of a sculptor's car
on sanitation trucks
on school bus windows
on fingers of a man picking his tooth
on coat of woman running with brown dog
on taxi cabs darting like yellow lizards to
avoid people waving in the rain
It's raining
& rocket launches are aborted in the rain
disgruntled employees go crazy in the rain
donut vendors fly up 7th Avenue in the rain
It's raining down on
black deep water umbrellas
on black & red Eshu umbrellas
on blood red Shango umbrellas
on honey gold Oshun umbrellas
on blue & white fertility umbrellas
on purple Ogun umbrellas
on melancholy green umbrellas
on the engineer of umbrellas it's raining
it's raining
at the drug & alcohol rehabilitation house
a brief afternoon downpour
splashes vomit on shoes of
one big shot censorship clerk
& a chilly hail pushes
untreated sewage into the sound
& It's raining

on midnight Island hoppers
on humorous strap hangers
on free love seats in the land fill
& rain has a wet ticket to paradise
rain has designer braces flashing
at the New York Secretary Show
rain is happy the rainbow has
a hole in its condom
rain is alive & storming with ecstasy
let's hear it for the rain

Neighbor

Neighbor

everyday

you get up

coughing

harking

screaming at the dog

cursing yourself out

& for what

you are there

you see something coming

the event happens

and you can't go back to the beginning

The Dreams

I close my eyes
miss the right train
board the wrong bus
get lost   get drunk
rub down in cactus juice
dress up in wild turkey feathers
walk with vodun priest
into horrible charcoal mist
of a government assassination building

I clear my throat
scratch my belly
drop into dream of deflated whales
into sockets of inflamed cobras
my thigh a fly swatter of dead flies
my forehead a tuning pipe of unmelodious pinging
my uterus an enlarged ball of electric piranhas

I move
& the hole in the rug becomes
a transparent river of crocodiles
I stand on head of this hippo
to check out the tornado
of musical instruments
& with a dizzy sadness in my chest
I scream   I swallow   I moan
I hold smoke in my navel
spit ink into
my imaginary microphone fist

I whisper   I cough
I see my desk & papers gone
my passport torn & crushed
my tennis shoes frozen in ice
one half madwoman with baby says
she's Ogotemmeli
& boom
an abrupt change of pitch

A dark cave of talking rocks
an enormous bed of snoring camels
the house of wounded skunk
the old outspoken eagle squawks coming
from stomach of an unsatisfied bankteller on fire
& the midget says
imagination smiles
like a fat prostitute
& the waitress swears she has
the meaning of life & death
wrapped in four plastic baggies
I grin & drink white lightning
mixed with fried cabbage
bury myself like a frog
hear intoxicated ancestors talking backward
& there are yellow cows
with broken hooves dangling against the sky
men with alligator meat packed on their knees
women with dream policies between teeth
horses with ripped ligaments in pockets
& I sit & I watch &
I search my speech impediment
for discharging passengers
I invert the swelter in one nostril

I leap for air like dolphins
I turn loose ritual of turning loose
on sand bags
my flesh waiting
to be invaded
by cold blooded lizards
my fish stained napkin
ready for confiscation
my empty shoes
available for adoption
the ghost in my hair stinking

Dear Banjo

Dear Banjo
I am staggering
like
unprofessional
exterminator
in fumes
blood shooting
toward me
in a flood of lights
cutting off
as I piss
& one pyramid splits

death shovels
walking from my vagina
xylophone keys puking
Beaujolais bottles exploding
turds overflowing
from toilet
of snake skin boots
my tongue
swallowing itself
in a bed of savage ants

Don't Ask/1980

Don't ask me
who I'm speaking for
who I'm talking to
why I'm doing what I do in
the light of my existence

You rise you spit you brush you drink you
pee you shit you walk you run you work
you eat you belch you sleep you dream &
that's the way it is

In the morning
tap water taste fishy
coffee sits in its
decaffeinated cup
ca ca & incense
have a floating romance
& a stale wash cloth
will make you smell
doubly stale so
don't get kissed on the cheek
don't get licked on the neck

at 8 AM
the trains & buses are
packed with folks farting
their bread & butter farts
the gymnasium
is dominated
by the stench of
hot tennis shoes

& in one locker room
a few silly talking
intellectual looking
coke drinking
cloth dropping
paper littering
spinach pooting
smug arrogant women wait to
be waited on

& in another locker room
there are odors of
crotches & jock straps
ben gay, tiger balm
& burning balls
sweat socks & sweat suits
of body building
door slamming
iron pumping
phlegm harking men
all sour & steamy
& wrapped up together
in a swamp of
butt popping towels
but don't let it
get you down
don't let it
psyche you up

Outside the ledges are
loaded with pigeons
clouds are seeded with
homeless people &
lyricism of the afternoon
is a sub-proletarian madman
squatting & vomiting
from his bowels
a brown liquid of death
in front of your house

   & it's not happening because of you
   those socks don't stink because of me
   a bureaucrat is not a jerk because of us
   I'm not this way because of them
   you're not that way because of me
   don't ask about influences

You rise you spit you brush you drink you
pee you shit you walk you run you work
you eat you belch you sleep you dream
& that's the way it is

Atmospheric Burn
for the Printmaking Workshop

A poem
of patriotic spitballs blowing
when the hour comes up
like flying saucer hairdo
>	sparkling until
>	five below zero
>	then commercial break

the move
into menopause of warm snakes
a peck
into lightning zone of smashed bananas
>	West of the big belch
>	of unfinished identities
>	& what did you expect

One sunrise
made of tomatoes & onions
Three poems
in porcupine skull under a wig in Harlem
Don't curse
it's cold in these red-stained ancestor trenches
Don't laugh
it's not so easy to reach
the upside-down tree rooted to
samba screeches of staggering shades
Don't shoot
arrest that dinosaur with the carbon monoxide breath
>	Look

the circle frozen in its black jade asphalt
rolls through my collagraphic mouth

the blossoming knots stand like
UFO tracings
on my monoprinting teeth
the flag waves in
foreskin of my bullet train fingers
        then a dose of caffeine
        an excess of poetic discharge
        a flamestorm from
        the next century of pimples
and once upon an atmospheric burn
the clock   the yawn   the commotion of paper voices

I Have Been Searching
(Rwanda Conflict)

I have been searching
and searching and searching
since the day they said
you were tossed into a ditch by
a bulldozer
I have been searching all the ditches
trying to find you beneath
a million human bones
I have been searching between
twenty thousand bandaged skulls
I have been searching in a town of
fifty thousand jagged wounds
I have been searching in the ashes and
searching in the bloody footprints
and oh my friend
I have found nothing but
the song of dying
and the song of not knowing
the song of dying
and the song of not knowing

I have been searching and
searching and searching
since the day they said
they saw you standing there when
the assassins came in
they said you didn't have a chance to hide
you didn't have time to run
they said they thought they saw

you standing there
and I have been searching
and searching and searching
and oh my friend
I have found nothing but
the sky all smoky with skin
the bulldozer of bones
the bloody footprints
and the factions within factions of factions of
factions of factions and
I have been searching but
I cannot find you anywhere
I have been searching and
searching and searching

To Chrysler Cirrus

Dear Chrysler Cirrus
Do not bother to schedule
a personal driving experience for me
in your luxury new coupe
I will not spread-eagle on your wheel
or let your corporation
fuck me in my ears
so you can hear the music better

I Wonder Who

We have been calling across fields
& falsetto snapping & moaning
in deep Shona deep Edo deep Mandingo
before the erection
of artificial systems

& we have been building granaries
pounding grain
going from dry stream
to dry stream
since the beginning of
the illumination of stars

We have been pulling tons of wood
up the road
in the rain
in malaria land
for thousands of years

& we have been ploughing across deserts
linking events
& circulating information
since the division of night & day
day & night

Now I wonder
I wonder who will tell
all the Presidents Ministers & Chiefs
that can't decontaminate anything
to click their boots together & scram

I wonder who will make it happen

I wonder who will tell
all the missionaries to put
their satellite systems of surveillance
on their two religious feet
& split on back to where they came from

I wonder who will make it happen

I wonder who will tell
all the non-serious
scholars & expert invaders of indigenous cultures
to take their little bright ideas
shove them down their own throats &
cancel the habit of spreading shit

I wonder who will make it happen

I wonder who will tell
all the mercenary units
to take their
festive blood sausage farts
& the inexhaustible volume of human greed
that stinks of Jonas Savimbi's sweat
& blow out of Africa

I wonder who will make it happen

I wonder who will take
all the savage attachés & ton ton macoutes
& put them with
the industrial waste
that's buried in the tropics

I wonder who will make it happen

I wonder who will tell
all the undemocratic afrikaaner trekkers
to have a good time
trekking on back to the Netherlands
& keep on trekking

I wonder who will make it happen

I wonder who will send
the bones of Cecil Rhodes
from Zimbabwe back to funk city in England
so the piranhas can have
a cannibalistic snack in front of
a topless princess on the Thames

I wonder why nobody ever did it

The Guitars I Used To Know

Guitars
with excavated rhythms
with maps & bridges
& the sweetness of sugar from
              Pernambuco
          from Nacogdoches
    from Itta Bena
from Chitunguiza
Guitars
with names like
   Edolia Adelia
     Freddie Mae Johnny Boy
Matakenya Machado
   Zodwa & Letty Bea
Guitars
Guitars full of
inlaid shark fins
apocalyptic blood-stained finger boards
intoxicated paradoxinated coils
indigenous fusionous realms
collisional digital switches
reverse reverb shrills on flat-bed trucks
   Guitars
The guitars trembling into
ultrasonic tempos into
insurrectional gestures into
scrunching wild dog yowls
Yowling
with the mother-of-pearl habit
of living in isolation

with the plastic tradition
of being too sociable
with the inflammatory projections
hyperventilating into
trances stances romances
Guitars
The guitars I used to know
Guitars
arriving from Chicago
from Takaradi
from Casamance
from Texas
from Toledo
  & I can hear
  the guitars calling themselves Lightnin'
  I can hear the guitars calling themselves T Bone
  I can hear the guitars calling themselves Minnie
  & I can hear the black laquered guitars
  & the red guitars & the big brown rusty guitars
  & cadillac green guitars & majestic purple guitars
  & metallic blue   Guitars
accoustically dipping down whispering
'Don't make me wait too long now'   Guitars
electronically screaming
'I heard you beating your lover last night'   Guitars
zigzagging through the crowd & shouting
'I'm not losing my mind over you baby'   Guitars
marching around & yelling
'I'm gonna cut your power line'   Guitars
turning flips & whining
like ritual killers   Guitars
vamping on bandstands
& laughing like howler monkeys   Guitars
clearing paths

& humming like violins from Swaziland   Guitars
hollering half tone half step higher than
ordinary catastrophes   Guitars
circling with strings on teeth & crying ouch
Guitars
gigless   strapless
hanging upside-down like
disembodied robots
between dilapidated flamenco boots
exhausted pubic bones
& torn alligator shoe tongues
Guitars
hanging upside-down while
people imitate specialty of
the next machine   Guitars hanging
upside-down before resurrecting & exploding
straight out into the air
of numb thumbs
of snap slaps
of steel squeals
of moan zones
of pecked necks
of drill trills
of joke smoke
of set frets
of ride slides
of squeeze freeze
of plunk funk
of ping ting
of jam slam slam slam slam slam
          slam slam slam
Guitars
The guitars I used to know

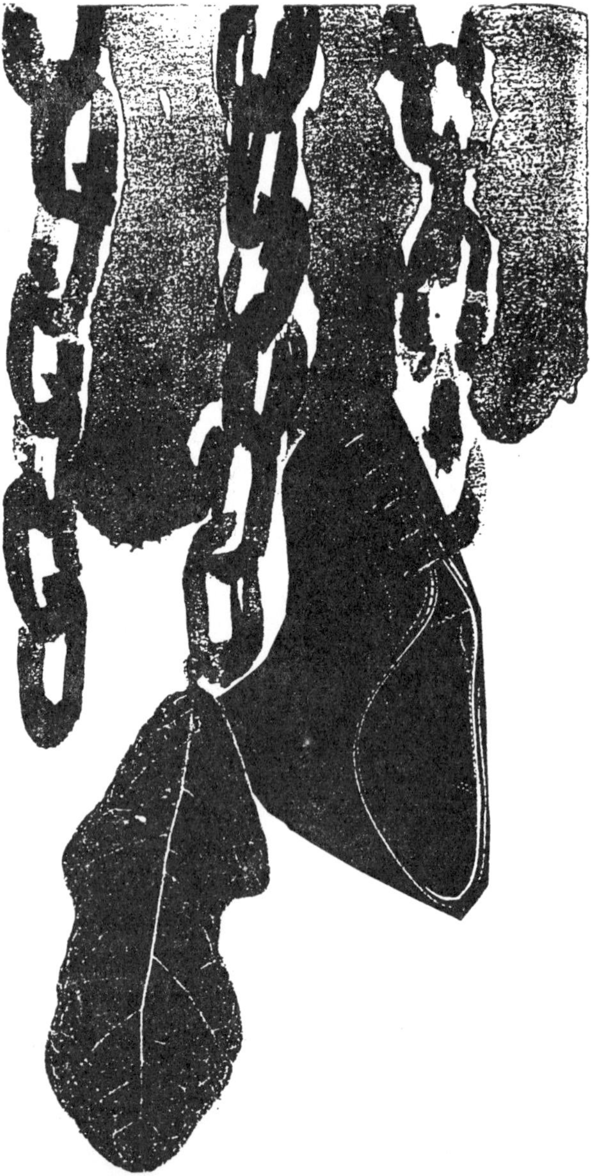

What Can We Sing for You

What can we sing
    for you
    that you
have not already
    sung
for yourself
in natural
supernatural setting
    of world songs

    we praise
your creativity
   & say
    someone
snatched your chance
    someone
murdered your luck
& without a doubt
there is no
right moment
for a solo
that happens
because
it hears
    itself
flying
before
taking
   a smoke

The Arrival

Again
the arrival
the exit
memories dissolving
in frisky butt
of a wild goat
Traditions
rolling into
tight balls
of fried snot
A manuscript
of dead looks
dead struggles
dead erections
in dead holes
of waterless
deserts
advancing
into deserts
property
merging
with property
Stocks
climbing
straight up
on a tremor
of bones
come storm
come sun
come drought

I Got the Blue-Ooze 93

I got the blue-ooze
I got the fishing in raw sewage blue-ooze
I got the toxic waste dump in my backyard blue-ooze
I got the contaminated drinking water blue-ooze
I got the man-made famine blue-ooze
I got the HIV AIDS epidemic blue-ooze
I got the dead house dead earth blue-ooze
I got the blue-ooze
I got the living in a drain-pipe blue-ooze
I got the sleeping in a cardboard box
    waiting for democracy to hit blue-ooze
I got the 5 hundred year black hostage
    colonialism never never stops blue-ooze
I got the francophone   anglophone   alementiphone
    lusophone telephone   blue-ooze
I got this terminology is not my terminology
    these low standards are not my standards
    this religion is not my religion and
    that justice has no justice for me blue-ooze
I got the blue-ooze
I got the gangbanging police brutality blue-ooze
I got the domestic abuse battered body blue-ooze
I got the ethnic conflict blue-ooze
I got the misinformation media penetration blue-ooze
I got the television collective life is no life to live
    and this world is really becoming
        a fucked up crowded place to be blue-ooze
  I got to find a way out this blue-ooze
because the blue-ooze
will make you sorry

that you ever had
the blue-oo-oo-ooze
I got the blue-ooze
I got the blue-oo-oo-ooze

Whatever Frightens

Whatever frightens
drunk crickets in dead reefer of your lungs
whatever fascinates alcoholic termites
on wooden tooth in your melancholy pimp mouth
whatever it is
the festival will start with
a twirling umbrella of rayon panties
a dark queendom of yawning vaginas
a urinating ear of hot asphalt words
that you can eat
in spanish fly of your french kiss
that you can swallow
in slobbering joy
of your snag nasty fear
that you can see
like a dance joking butt in the air
so please clear the street
of your broken teeth at once

Why Not
(Babs Gonzales)

    Why not
    let Babs
    dominate
    this night
    with his
    thirty year
    rite of
        oo bop sha bam
Horns imitating him
as he imitated them
in up tempo grooveness
        of Expubidence
a riffology collaboration
    a sha ba dah ba doot doot
    in front of
sheel-lee-ah doo bee dah
    rejection into
    an injection of
oo daba doo bay doo yey doo yey doo
    Itself
    a home
    demonstration
    of those
    flat sharp
    natural sensations
    swinging
    at the end of the wind
    of a big ole nasty
    tenor saxophone ya ya ya yawl lapowl

    and why not

    Why not
    let Babs
    drop his
bitter stream dream elaborations
    his
gravely back throat stroke of
       bold premonitions
    his
fermented chest rest nest of
unvomited insurrections
    into
bopology explanations
tongue blistering configurations
confrontations quotations
    in celebration
    of those
    metal tipped
    melodious drips
    in lips
    on fire
    after midnight
       and why not

    Why not
    let Babs
    leave
    his hot
    orikiisms
in bandstand blood of the blues
in amber lights of city tubes

oo ya cooing and oop pop a dahing
   on his way to
   ee ee ee doo blah blee
   blee blah doo ee ee ee ee ee
      and why not

The Oppressionists

Art
what do the art
suppressors
care about art
they jump on bandwagons
wallow in press clips
& stink up the planet
with their
pornographic oppression
Art
what do they care about art
they go from being
contemporary baby kissers to
old time corrupt politicians
to self-appointed censorship clerks
who won't support art
but will support war
poverty
lung cancer
racism
colonialism
& toxic sludge
that's their morality
that's their religious conviction
that's their protection of the public
& contribution to family entertainment
what do they care about art

I'm Gonna

I'm gonna shake like a violent rain storm
I'm gonna fill the night with splashing
I'm gonna sit like a zone of confluence
I'm gonna gallop in the inner basin
I'm gonna drink from the new molasses
I'm gonna rub my body with palm oil
I'm gonna stuff my bones with charcoal
I'm gonna paint myself with arrows
I'm gonna click my bottles together
I'm gonna zigzag over & under
I'm gonna reach for the solar cycle
I'm gonna swirl up through the rapids
I'm gonna wail & point the wailings
I'm gonna stand like wall of protection
I'm gonna move like a desert darkness
I'm gonna push out further & further
I'm gonna press in closer & closer
I'm gonna dive down deeper & deeper
I'm gonna kick up higher & higher & higher

A Miles Davis Trumpet

There are the ivory trumpets from Africa
the silver trumpets found in drawings
on walls of Egyptian tombs
telescoping trumpets from China
trumpets that live in Tibet
spanish speaking trumpets of Spain
& then
there is
that trumpet
with solitary feeling of sound
splashing through rough woodshed of Charlie Parker
splashing the sound of distance
                    in trumpet
                    against orchestra
trumpet circling within box
            of a box
                of controlled settings
    trumpet
patinaed with layers of rust & spit
grooving inside the groove surface
trumpet
with bell of funk fired up
in middle extremities
between bass & treble
thunder & whistle
Unmuzzled cheeks of brass
inflated storm of mutes
elastic electric Elegba
that trumpet

There are the oceanic shell trumpets
buzzing Southern Indian trumpets
natural Arabian trumpets
fast talking Cuban trumpets
European inspired valve trumpets
trumpets with great ears
& husky tones & avant garde ways
trumpets fanfaring   dirging   parading
& giving military salutes

There are
side-blown trumpets
side-winder trumpets
straight trumpets
sweet trumpets
Satchmo trumpets
Oliver trumpets
Bolden trumpets
Little Jazz trumpets
Red trumpets
Rex trumpets
Dorham trumpets
curved trumpets
Dizzy trumpets
Clark trumpets
Hot Lip trumpets
Fat trumpets
pocket trumpets
Cootie trumpets
Farmer trumpets
Brownie trumpets
Cherry trumpets
& then there is

that short dark popping trumpet
covered in a mask of
New York hipness & fame
that trumpet
with another hairdo
another change of aspirations
another half nelson in
a constellation of dust
another motif in
    terry cloth turban
another hoarse voice of
Orin to ti Orunwa
that trumpet

That trumpet
with the sound of chance
the sound of prediction
the sound of invention
the sound of migration & madness
& fluidity of solitude
& mathematical flurries
& blasted bridges
& dynamism within
collectivity of the hunt
that trumpet
with jom
with spirit
with secret sound systems hidden
behind sun glass fetishes
that trumpet
has a throat
which sits outside
of its body

sits on top of the wind
on top of the band
with explosive pucks
mystical rain spittle
aboriginal tongue toot toots
that trumpet
that trumpet is
the militant   mellow   melodic   magical
miraculous   minimalist   Miles Davis trumpet
that trumpet

So What

So what
if I spend
the rest of my life
living on invisible mouth
of an imaginary saxophone
      breathing in
      & blowing out
      polluted airs
      in August
doo bee   doo bee   doo bee   suck suck
all the way through this tunnel
   so what
   if you sniff
the monumental torture smell of power
            like
toe jam   piss   & rotten cabbage
on sleeves of my last overcoat
      don't jump off
      throw up
      fall down
I want you
to touch my hair like
      so many flies
understand these boogers I eat
      don't worry
        it's the business of death
      to be hungry
I only sit
in its lap like

a buzzard
one lick at a time
      doo bee   doo bee   doo bee   suck suck

The Harmattan

Midnight special
throbbing through smells of the harmattan

On night
of the shaking tambourines
the night I loved you
while standing like Sierra Madre

Sperms backed up
in your feet
to your head
        ten days strong

Midnight special
throbbing through smells of the harmattan

& I saw
the sun falling
like tray of tin spoons
belly dancers
        low-riding in dust
star beer
        splashing through fog
your ass moonshining
        like diamond igloo
down in smoked brown night
of cross current tongues
fingers of another bongo player on fire

Midnight special
throbbing through smells of the harmattan

There Are No Stars

There are no stars
no sky   no moon
in this city tonight

Everything is afterbirth acid of
bird urine on
that dark seance sea of air
that excessively
oxidized torso
posing in a pool
of fierce ash eruptions

the sunset bleeding like menstruating chimpanzee
Blood splattered sutures of intoxicated clouds

& I am this city's planet
this evening's massive thigh of swelter
this comb of cock
this stomach of archeological digs
this mixture of may fly & carp
there are no other late summer
early autumn
spectacle of lights

Bumblebee, You Saw Big Mama

You saw Big Mama Thornton
in her cocktail dresses
& cut off boots
& in her cowboy hat
& man's suit
as she drummed &
hollered out
the happy hour of her negritude
                        Bumblebee

You saw Big Mama
trance dancing her chant
into cut body of
a running rooster
scream shouting her talk
into flaming path of
a solar eclipse
cry laughing her eyes into
circumcision red sunsets
                   at midnight
                Bumblebee

You saw Big Mama
bouncing straight up like a Masai
then falling back spinning her
salty bone drying kisser of music
into a Texas hop for you to
lap up her sweat
                Bumble Bee

You saw Big Mama
moaning between ritual saxes
& carrying the black water of Alabama blood
through burnt weeds & rainy ditches
to reach the waxy surface of your spectrum
       Bumblebee

You didn't have to wonder
why Big Mama sounded
so expressively free
so aggressively great
once you climbed
into valley roar
of her vocal spleen
& tasted sweet grapes
in cool desert
of her twilight
   Bumblebee

You saw Big Mama
glowing like
a full charcoal moon
riding down
Chocolate Bayou road
& making her entrance
into rock-city-bar lounge
& swallowing that
show-me-no-love supermarket exit sign
in her club ebony gut
you saw her
get tamped on by the hell hounds
& you knew when she was happy
you knew when she was agitated

you knew what would make her thirsty
you knew why Big Mama
heated up the blues for Big Mama
to have the blues with you
   after you stung her
    & she chewed off your stinger
       Bumblebee
     You saw Big Mama

Me

Me
I'm gonna put
these partial dentures
    on ice
spit one last spit on
hammer ringing zing
fly over the moon
    in front of
      the Dew-Drop Inn
& when
the odorific quicksand
the water fleas
the jelly snot
& shadow hawks
    show up
like human babies
covered with brown snails
    I'm gonna cross over
      push back
        gyrate
         & blow
           my fishtail wind
            in their faces

Global Inequalities

Chairperson of the board
is not digging for roots
        in the shadows
There's no dying-of-hunger stare
        in eyes of
Chief executive officer of petroleum
Somebody else is sinking into
        spring freeze of the soil
Somebody else is evaporating
        in dry wind of the famine
there's no severe drought
        in mouth of
Senior vice president of funding services
No military contractor is sitting
        in heat of a disappearing lake
No river is drying up
        in kidneys of
        a minister of defense
Under-secretary of interior
    is not writing distress signals
        on shithouse walls
Do you see refugee camp cooped up
        in head of
Vice president of municipal bonds
There's no food shortage
        in belly of
        a minister of agriculture
Chief economic advisors are
            addicted to diet pills
Banking committee members are

                suffering from obesity
Somebody else is sucking on dehydrated nipples
Somebody else is filling up on fly specks
The Bishops are not
            forcing themselves to eat bark
The security exchange commission members
            are sick from
            too many chocolate chip cookies
The treasury secretary
            is not going around in circles
              looking for grain
There's no desert growing in nose of
            Supreme commander of justice
It's somebody else without weight
without blood without land
without a cloud cover of water on the face
It's somebody else
Always somebody else

Compañera
(Ana Mendieta)

Compañera
We should have bolted you down like
a piece of iron sculpture and
pointed you in another direction
but you were busy looking for love
in the wrong dictionary
looking for a sweet papa
in the wrong encyclopedia

& now I say to myself
Ana is dead
not alive
not returning
what would she think of that

She arrived in the Apple
to jog around the park
have lunch with friends
create sculpture
install exhibitions
& get intellectual stimulation from
a drunk lover who swears
he did not throw her
out of the window
so why say
performance artist takes a dive
political thinker leaves in a huff
short intense Cuban shows her anger
big orphan mouth sculptor leaps

Ana did not leap
because Ana knew
Ana could not fly

So why not say
her breath was filled
with black beans
green tomatoes
mojitos & Guantanamera
with garlic
cervesa
cilantro
the sweet melodies of Beny Moré
River Oshun foam
dark Havana rum splashes
& the water running rhythms of
Orquesta Aragon

Why not say
She was carver of wood and earth
collector of Cuban jokes
a cyclone in blue tennis shoes
a sequin dress machete
forever cutting through the
dry thunder of oppression
&
it was no dream when she yelled
'that chauvinist shit
that stinking little bitch
that phony bastard with his
fucking elite whores
& his kissing lips full of smoking ass
sucking on this corrupt spirit-breaking system

of fucked up interventionist agendas'
It was no dream
So why not say
if a short rainbow
signifies in face
of an outbreak of pink marble flames
there will be blood
in hair of the dirt storm
& if respect is a somber silueta
etched in consciousness of a warm cave
there will be an erection of hate
in eurocentric bones
if a conspirator plots
& you cannot overthrow or float
the navel will never know its umbilical future

Why not say
after the exit of two great drummers
& in between the entrance of
one monumental earthquake
a huge volcano eruption
& reappearance of the tail of Halley's comet
We lost Ana

but Ana did not leap
because Ana knew
Ana could not fly

Be Good Enough

Be good enough
not to pee with the jackals
you speak radiation real well
your pronunciations sound like
crushed fire engines in the nose
who cares what
an embalmer drinks
    I'm in favor of
    flushing toilets
    flooding nights
    & moving through
    the outskirts of nowhere
    to make this matter more than
    suddenly immediately
    & thank you very much for coming

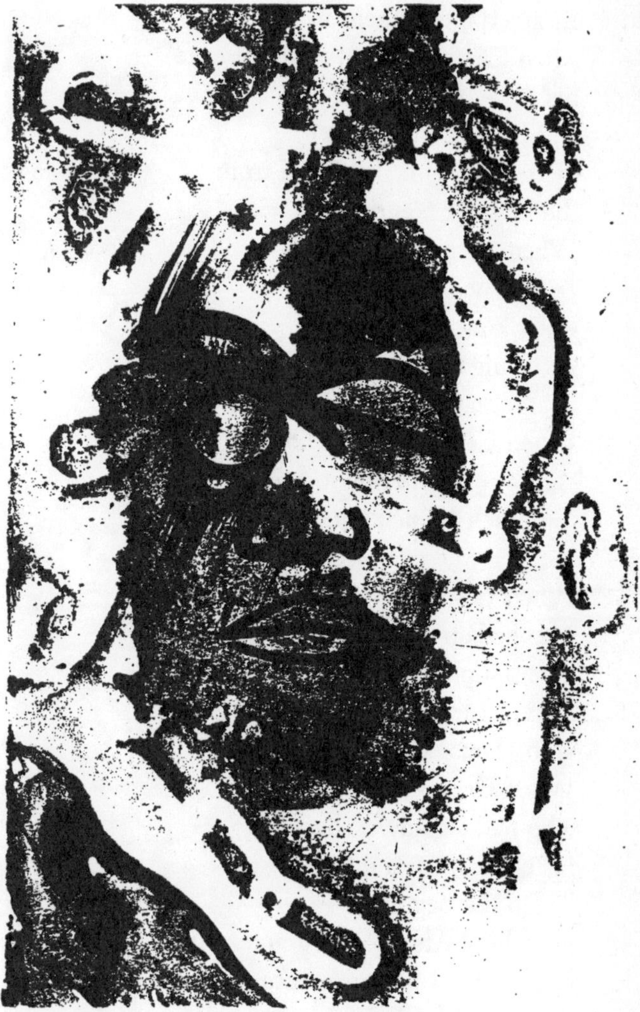

At a Certain Moment in History

At a certain moment in history
when Césaire started to decolonize
his neo-colonial head
and free his image
by dealing with the world from
the ideas of Negritude
When young Aimé Césaire said fuck Paree
& returned
to look into the future
by diving inside the past of
              his native land
When Césaire arrived home to
clarify the contradictions of
too much French wine in
the wee wee of Martinique
When Césaire
who had already incorporated
his multiple rhythms into
the African rhythm section
with Damas & Senghor
When Césaire
who had already exchanged
his clarinet for a drum
began the beguine
in style of Atumpan drummers
& sang until his voice became
the agitated volcano mouth
              of calamities
It was no exotic voodoo movie script
no get down deep in the Congo poetry slam

It was Césaire
> returning to
a forest of dangerous plants
A forest even home boys didn't enter
without revolutionary intentions
& at that moment of no compromise
his poetry became poetry unique to poetry
his long lava flowing lines moved
beyond classification & geographical links
He fired up words that revolted like
overheated cockroaches
his notebook was the advancement on the path &
sharp point on the spear
He made poetic revolutionary cuts

Now I Dig Up Patinas

Now I dig up patinas
I chew on slit logs
I polish surfaces of cyclones
I mount bullet wounds to inspect
mutilations
I uproot the spirit of
the chemicals that make me
violate myself
I count limited resources
I view sink holes in
the atmosphere
I lubricate the batas
& provoke in all keys of
flesh & hallucinogenic gongs
the obscenities stuck to
my elbow of whistling bones
& with Olmec sculptors shrieking through
banana grove of my solitude
at 12:45 AM
& with the jaguars dropping from
my throat
& with the pumice of bulldog ants rising from
my damp discharge zone of
poetic fission
& with medicinal fat of
a big time rooster
in my nose of talkative boogers
& with torn crows flying from my
brown bearded ovum of
sulfuric acid blood

& with the insects blowing from
my colon of atomic leaves
& with mescal tears of oppressed fleas
smeared on wings
of my ovarian cysts
I detonate
I nuclear react
I frenzy faces of
fascist thought
I become
Zaire River mouth
pissing on every
corrupt officer in an old
leopard skin Mobutu Sese Seku cap
I unmuzzle my
black stretched limousine lips
I say
I'm a poet
to vin rouge
vin blanc
drunk fly
corpse of a roach in a cup

She Got He Got

She got hot
got happy   got hot
got thrilled   got hot
got degreed   got hot
got silly   got hot
got possessive   got hot
got disappointed   got hot
got hurt   got hot
got nurtured   got hot
got bitter   got hot
got drunk   got hot
got drugged   got hot
got rastered   got hot
got pregnant   got hot
got rejected   got hot
got indifferent   got hot
got lost   got hot
got born again   got hot again
got political again   got hot again
got academically ambitious again   got hot again
got hot   hot   hot   again
got to be a hot skeleton in the latest hot fashion
got hot
got to be a hot feminist turning into
a hot cultural investigative gadfly   got hot
got to be a hot exile flying
into alcoholic tantrums on hot buses   got hot
got to be a hot four hundred pound baby doll
becoming a real hot sociable walking disease with
a pretty hot face   got hot

she got hot   she got sad
she got hot   she got crazy
she got hot   she got athletic
she got hot   she got impatient
she got hot   she got used
she got hot without sweat   she got hot
she got hot without heat   she got hot
she got hot like a hot young volcano
got hot
got hot like a hot old bubbling crater
got hot
got hot and got to screaming 'rescue me'
got hot and got to shouting 'open the door Richard'
got hot and got bound to a sewing machine
got hot and got glued to a cash register
got hot and got tied to a computer
got hot and got stuck on the global assembly line
she got hot   she got hot hot   she got hot
she got aggressive   she got hot
she got bored   she got hot
she got frigid   she got hot
she got harassed   she got hot
she got depressed   she got hot
she got angry   she got hot
she got hot and so much alone and hot
and so inwardly focused and hot
and numb and hot and raw and hot and
so unprepared to be so hot and
so limited and hot and so dominated by the
thought of being so hot
all because a certain person didn't say
'I will love you forever baby'
she got hot   she got hot   she got hot

He got   He got
He got cold
he got happy before he got cold
he got fed before he got cold
he got excited before he got cold
he got broken-hearted and warlike
and then he got cold   he got cold   he got cold
got self-righteous   got cold
got distorted   got cold
got authoritative   got cold
got cold and got to going berserk in the workplace
got cold and got to pimping in the projects
got cold and got to screaming for revenge
got cold and got to handing out punishments
got cold and got to setting up
situations that would fail   got cold   got cold
got frustrated   got cold
got no recognition   got cold
got high   got cold   got forgotten   got cold
he got cold
he got cold cold cold
he got cold
got cold like a cold mercenary   got cold
got cold like a cold hyper-fastidious
hotel manager   got cold
he got cold like a cold militarized
supervisor of clerks   got cold
got cold like a cold political hustler in the street
got cold
got cold like a cold over-the-hill CIA agent
got cold   he got cold   he got cold
he got cold   cold   cold
He got cold

he got cold without having ever
imagined that he'd be so cold & wooden &
cold & untropical & cold & plastic & cold &
mute & cold & ferocious & cold & rigid & cold
& cold while watching the sunshine &
cold while kissing himself in the mirror &
cold & removed & cold & swollen &
cold & dependent on being so cold
he got cold he got cold
he got cold & got to screaming
'it's a man's world'
got cold & got to hiphopping like a peacock
got cold & got to hollering 'I'm a macho man'
got cold & got glued to a subway booth
got cold & got tied to a department of sanitation
got cold & got pinned to a patrol car
got cold & got taped to a bar stool
got cold & got engaged to a pawn shop
got cold & got married to a race track
got cold
got critically cold
got artistically cold
got miscellaneously cold
got cold
got cold & so outwardly focused
& cold & mean & cold & greedy & cold & selfish
& cold & so concerned about appearing to be
so cold
all because somebody stole his lollipop
& no one could chip through the ice
to say 'I'll love you forever baby don't be so cold'
    he got cold
    he got cold   cold   cold
    he got cold

The Heavy Headed Dance
for Mel & Ted

I am dancing &
on my head
is the spotted skunk
whose scent did not protect it
from Mr. & Mrs. Archibald of Texas

On my head
is the stuffed bobcat
whose facial expression was set
by the taxidermy department

On my head
is a bull caught
in the act of masturbation
& on top of that
rides the moose
stunned-gunned while wading in a lake
& on top of that
are the monkeys
entrapped while urinating
& on top of that
lay the hyena
jackal & vulture
shot while eating from zebra carcasses
& on top of that
sits the ram with
largest horn on record
donated by Henry Beck

& with all the stuffed animals piled on my head
I am dancing past
lyricist with the baboon heart

I am dancing like a dog
in front of financial consultant
implanted with pig genes

I am dancing & fluttering like a butterfly
across from novelist posing
in a beaver skin coat

I am dancing near the astronomer
who circles the floor with her
uplifted face frozen like a tiger

I am dancing against window
of artificial coyotes
& howling with contemporary African band
in the grizzly bear room

I am dancing my pangolin hairdo dance
past the river of ants in panties
of gyrating vocal groups

I am dancing so many different dances
with so many bloated animals
dead on my head
that my head is
a dancing museum of unnatural history
& I am dancing where I cannot see
myself dancing to know

why I am dancing
but I am dancing
I am dancing

The Gulf Tones

It's
the importation
      of water bottles
        & missiles
the great demand
  for symbols
Henry the 8th & Othello
     dressed in battle fatigues
Aladdin rising with
     his polluted lamps of oil
Valentino soaked
     in camouflage cream
the thrill tent
     A W O L
    inside
  the patriot
   & scud
        fuck show

Get that lubricating jelly out of your helmet soldier

Say It

Say it
    and peel off that
        grey iguana skin mask
Say it
    & clean out your cockpit of
        intoxicated spiders
tear the sexual leaves of grief from your heart
pluck feathers of nostalgia from your nipples
push the slow moving masochistic mud slide of
    contralto voices
from your afternoon skull of anxiety   Say it
& let the tooth chips fall from
your hole or rebellious itches
let the excremental mountain of bones
shoot out from your ten farting poems in
the fly season   Say it
because everything is like an ambush
everything is like an incursion
flesh smoking flesh in
hemp field of
a fifty minute breakdown
time sodomizing time
in circular tunnel of asphalt & ashes
space revolting against space
in roar of an artillery salvo fuck   Say it
    & leave it splattered on mortuary of the moon
        reflective sap of dead weight
    store it in your propane bucket of memory
        sporadic tremblations of fear
    shove it into saliva of a roach

            radula of teeth between ovums
     throw it from your spine of excessive heat
          fertility smoke of fumigated funk
   talk to yourself in automobile of the clitoris
        soul of so much humanistic lip
Say it
& let pissy sheets of repression emerge
   from your breasts of paregoric flamingos
let crematorial paste
   in your solitary carcass of drums
    push through vaginal acidity of your bodega
     Say it
& plunge from invisibility of your camouflage
slide on fingernail filth
of your own larvae of triteness
be honorary shithead
in your own mouthful of erected statues
break through your own face
of accumulated door slams bam bam bam bam

Last night
I dreamt
Buddy Bolden threw
his horn
into Ponchartrain Lake
when I put
my name
under
every eyelid
every anthill
every bird wing
every mask of reptilian skin
drying in

the sun
so say it
forget it
& have a drop of grappa
the frog spits through the uterus in December

Don't Write

Don't write
    another word
      about wanting
        to write
          another word
        it's useless
the windows are filthy
the instruments contaminated
the smell of someone entering you
in shoes covered with turkey shit is here
            & what can you say
        this is not
          a great performance
        today is tomorrow
      I poot on your fax
    I piss on your xerox
I ca ca on your e-mail

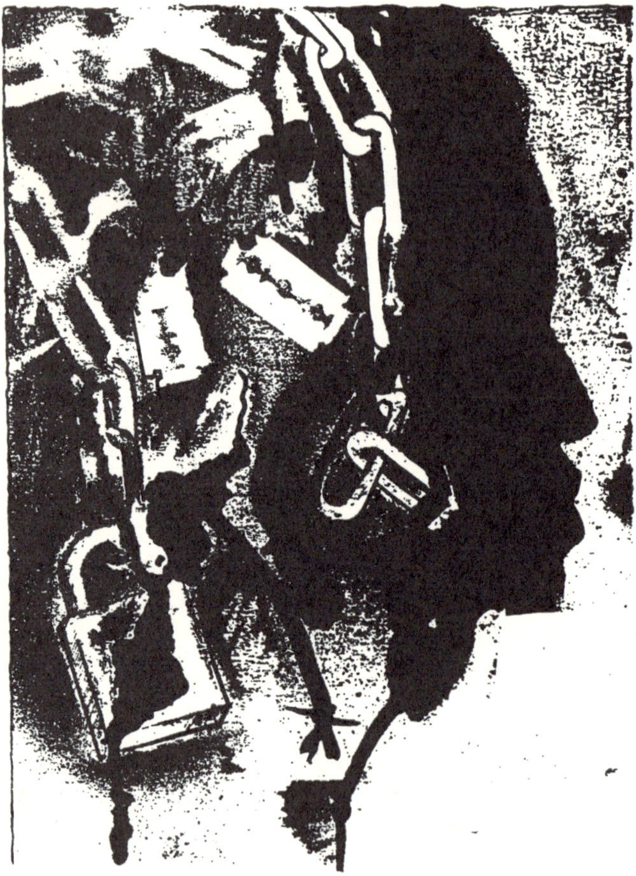

Sacred Trees

Every time I think about us women
I think about the trees   the trees
escaping from an epidemic of lightning
the sacred trees exploding from the
compressed matter of cuckoo spit   trees
the raped trees flashing signals through the
toxic acid of sucking insects
the trees used as decoy installations   trees

I have the afternoon leaves throbbing
        in my nostrils
I have the struggling limbs sprouting from
        these ear lobes
I have a power stump shooting from
        out of this forehead
I have clusters of twigs popping from
        my tattooed moles
& sometimes I feel
like the tree trunk
growing numb & dead
from ritual behavior
sometimes I feel like the tree ripping
from the core of ancient grievances
    Trees
I feel like
the family tree
relocating under pressure
    Trees
I feel like the frantic tree
trying to radiate through

    scorched surfaces
sometimes I feel like
the obscure tree
babbling through the silver-plated mouth
   of a shrinking moon
& sometimes I feel like a tree
hiccuping through
the heated flint of gunpowder crevices
sometimes I feel like a tree
& every time I think about us women
I think about the trees
I think about
the subversive trees laden in blood
        but not bleeding
the rebellious trees encrusted
        but not cracking
the abused trees wounded
        but still standing
I think about the proud trees
the trees with beehive tits buzzing
the transparent trees
the trees with quinine breath hovering
the trees swaying & rubbing their
stretched marked bellies
        in the rain
the crossroad trees coming from
       the tree womb
         of tree seeds
          Trees
I think about the trees
& sometimes I feel like
a superstitious tree
smelling negative & fragile

        & full of dislocated sap
sometimes I feel like
the tree stampeding from
        a cadre of earth tremors
I feel like the forgotten tree
    that can't live here no more
sometimes I feel
  like the tree that's growing wild
through the wild life left
in the petroleum pipeline
        I feel like a tree
A tree caught
in the catacomb of bones
        enslaved in
the red light districts of oppression
I feel like a barricade of trees
   I feel like a tree
& sometimes
I feel like the tree
that's lucky to be a tree
    in the time of
        missing trees
I feel like a tree
that's happy to be a tree
among disappearing trees
    Trees
I feel beautiful
    like an undestroyed
    rain forest of trees
I feel like a tree
  laughing in the rawness
     of the wind
I feel like a tree

& every time I think about us women
    I think about the trees
    I think about the trees

States of Motion

Sun Ra left the planet traveling in a pyramid made of
    metal keys
Willie Mae Thornton sailed away in an extra large
    moisture-proof harmonica
Pauline Johnson flew off to the meeting in her brass
    trimmed telephone
Thelonious Monk withdrew seated in a space ship
    shaped like a piano
Art Blakey departed in a great wood & stainless steel
    bass drum
Esther Phillips bowed out in a nasal sounding chrome
    microphone
Charles Tyler, George Adams & Clifford Jordan
    reached another realm riding in receptacles
    constructed like saxophones
Okot p'Bitek shoved off in an attache case full of
    songs, books & whiskey
Leon Damas hit the road in a big black banjo
Audre Lorde departed while wrapped in her book
    jackets
Dizzy Gillespie zoomed off in a sweet chariot shaped
    like a trumpet
Miles Davis left in a magnificent copper mute
Marietta Damas vacated the terrain in one beautiful
    house filled with folkloric & electronic gadgets
Romare Bearden crossed over the rainbow in a blimp
    made of his collages & etchings
Norman Lewis pushed away from the shore in a vault
    shaped like a bicycle

Ed Blackwell concealed in an assortment of cymbals
   march off to the Mardi Gras
Tchikaya U'Tamsi floated away in a big heart-shaped
   tuba
Vivian Browne departed draped in her painted forest
   canvases
Larry Neal went to the bush enclosed in two
   bookcases of poetry & Bebop tapes
Kimako Baraka evacuated the surface in a stone temple
   marked with Egyptian hieroglyphics
Wilfred Cartey got away from the hurricane in an
   ocean liner made of rum bottles
Johnny Makatini took off in a black, green & yellow
   rocket
Kathy Collins departed in a container made of
   unedited film clips
John Carter left in a fabulous silver clarinet
Evan Walker split in his boat that was shaped like a
   bird
Dumile Feni hurried to South Africa in one of his
   muscle-bound wooden sculptures
Peter Tosh reached the intersection in a bus filled with
   herbs & political newspapers
Bob Marley retreated away in a booming amplifier
   draped in African flags tied with dreadlocks
Ana Mendieta made her exit as a bronze Silueta
Michael Smith left for the forest in one huge audio
   cassette case
Elena & Jawa Apronti traveled from Accra in
   compartments made of ceremonial umbrellas
Bill Majors rode off into the sunset in a highly polished
   brass mercedes benz

Coco Anderson went to the festival in a fixture shaped
 like a yam wrapped with eight patchwork quilts
Franco L. Makiadi rolled off in a king-size purple
 guitar
Nicolás Guillén went to the rendezvous in a grand
 rumba cow bell
Tamu Bess traveled home in a queen-size computer
 plastered with eyeglasses
Flora Nwapa crossed the horizon concealed in pages
 of her new novel
Sarah Vaughan ascended in a misty glass recording
 booth
Gilberto de La Nuez disappeared into one of his
 paintings in Havana

Find Your Own Voice

Find your own voice & use it
use your own voice & find it

The sounds of drizzle
on dry leaves are not
like sounds of insults
between pedestrians

Those women laughing
in the window
do not sound like
air conditioners on the brink

The river turtle
does not breathe like
a slithering boa constrictor

The roar of a bull
is not like
the cackle of a hyena

The growl of a sea-leopard
is not like the teething cry
of a baby

The slash of a barracuda
is not like
the gulp of a leaping whale

The speech of a tiger shark
is not like
the bark of an eagle-fish

The scent of a gardenia
is not like the scent of a tangerine

Find your own voice & use it
use your own voice & find it

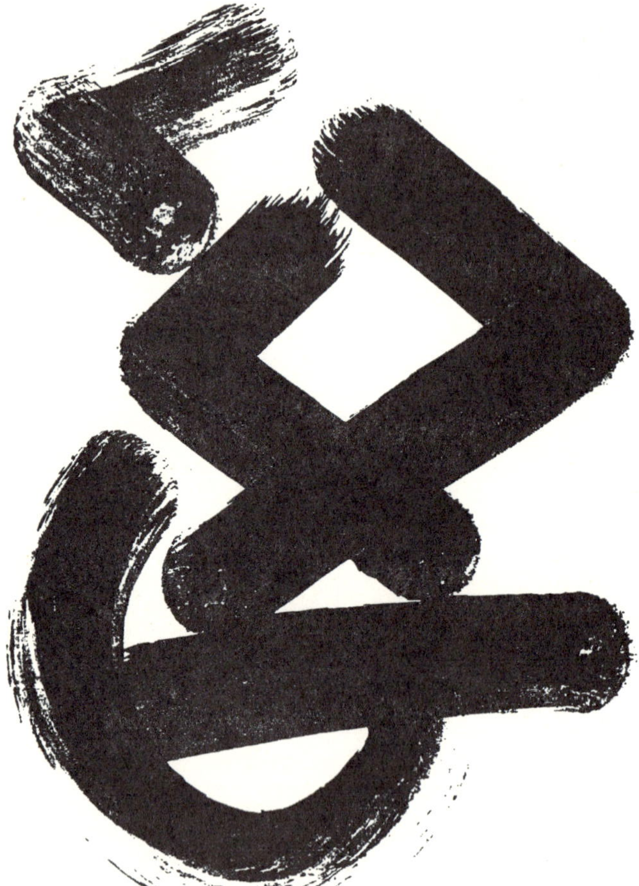

Glossary

ABEOKUTA: A city in Nigeria.
ADUPE: Thanks in the Yoruba language of Nigeria.
AIMÉ CESAIRÉ: Poet and writer from Martinique.
ANA MENDIETA: Cuban sculptor who died in New York City in 1985.
ANTONIO MACEO: The most celebrated general in Cuba's War of Independence 1868.
ASILAH: A town in Morocco.
BABALÁWO: Priest of Yoruba Ifa divination in Nigeria, Brazil, Cuba.
BABS GONZALES: One of the original Bebop Jazz vocalists.
BAYAMO: A Cuban city.
BATIDAS: Brazilian cocktail.
BENY MORÉ: Cuban singer.
WILLIE MAE "BIG MAMA" THORNTON: Singer of the blues.
BUDDY BOLDEN: Trumpet player from New Orleans.
CACHACA: White rum of Brazil.
CAPOIERA: African contest game played in Brazil.
CAPRINHAS: Brazilian cocktail.
CANDOMBLE: An Afro-Brazilian religion.
CHITUNGUIZA: A township of Harare, Zimbabwe.
COMMUNEDADO MANGUEIRA: A community in Rio de Janeiro.
EDO: An African language spoken in Edo State of Nigeria.
EFIK: A group of people and language in the Calabar district of Nigeria.

EGBAS: A group of Yorubas in Nigeria and Brazil.
ELEGBA: A Yoruba deity.
EWE: A group of people and language in Ghana and Togo.
EXU or ESHU: A Yoruba deity.
EXPUBIDENCE: Bebop linguistics used by Babs Gonzales.
FAVELA: A slum in Brazil.
FEIJOADA: A popular Brazilian dish made of black beans.
FULA: A West African language.
GE GE: A group of African people living in Brazil.
GUAGUA: Bus in Cuba.
GUANTANAMERA: A Cuban song.
GUARANA: Herbal stimulant in Brazil.
GULLA: Creolized English spoken in South Carolina.
HOPI: A group of Native American people living in the United States.
ITTA BENA: A town in Mississippi.
JONAS SAVIMBI: Unita leader responsible for a war against the people of Angola.
JOSÉ CLEMENTE OROZCO: Mexican muralist.
JESUŚ MENENDEZ: Cuban labor leader assassinated in 1948.
JOSÉ MARTI: Cuban patriot and founder of the Cuban revolutionary party.
MALECON: Ocean front promenade and drive in Havana.
MANDINGO: A group of people and language in Sierra Leone and Gambia.
MASAI: A group of people in East Africa.
MAU MAU: Revolutionaries in colonial Kenya.
MBIRA: African hand piano.

MENDE: A group of African people and language in Sierra Leone.

MONCADA BARRACKS: The garrison attacked in 1953, recognized as the start of the Cuban Revolution.

MOSSI: A group of people and language in Burkina Faso.

MUQUECA: An Afro-Brazilian dish.

NACOGDOCHES: A town in Texas.

NAVAHO: Native American people in the United States.

NEGRISMO: 1930s literary movement in Cuba.

NICOLÁS GUILLÉN: National poet of Cuba.

OGOTEMMELI: Philosopher and historian of the Dogon people in Mali.

OGUN: Yoruba deity of iron and war in Nigeria, Cuba, and Brazil.

OKO: Yoruba deity of agriculture in Nigeria, Cuba, and Brazil.

ORIN TO TI ORUNWA: The sound from heaven, in the Yoruba language.

ORISHA: Name for Yoruba deities.

OXALA: Yoruba deity of the sky in Brazil.

OXUM or OSHUN: Yoruba Goddess of the Oshun river in Nigeria.

PAPAGO: Native American people in the United States.

PERNAMBUCO: A state in Brazil.

PERFIL: Profile in Portuguese.

RARA: A festival in Haiti.

REI: King in Portuguese.

ROQUETS: Bar in Paris, France.

SAMBA: Brazilian music and dance.

SANTERIA: Synthesis of African religions.
SANTI SPIRITUS: Cuban city.
SHANGO or XANGO: Yoruba deity of thunder and lightning.
SHONA: A group of people and language in Zimbabwe.
TONTON MACOUTE: Name for the independent security forces established by Francois Duvalier in Haiti.
TWI: An African language spoken in Ghana.
VATAPA: A Brazilian dish.
VODUN: A religion in the Republic of Benin and Haiti.
WILFREDO LAM: A Cuban painter.
VEDADO: An area in Havana.
YEMAYA: The Yoruba goddess of the sea.
YORUBA: A group of people and language originating in Nigeria.

Ghost of Chance
  William S. Burroughs
  1-85242-406-0

Minus Time
  Catherine Bush
  1-85242-408-7

Tricks
  Renaud Camus
  1-85242-414-1

Somewhere in Advance of Nowhere
  Jayne Cortez
  1-85242-422-2

Endf of the Story
  Lydia Davis
  1-85242-420-6

Break It Down
  Lydia Davis
  1-85242-421-4

Powerless
  Tim Dlugos
  1-85442-407-9

You Got to Burn to Shine
  John Giorno
  1-85242-321-8

Margery Kempe
  Robert Glück
  1-85242-334-X

Jack the Modernist
  Robert Glück
  1-85242-333-1

To the Friend Whho Did Not Save My Life
  Hérve Guibert
  1-85242-328-5

Slow Death
    Stewart Home
    1-85242-519-9

Rent Boy
    Gary Indiana
    1-85242-324-2

Gone Tomorrow
    Gary Indiana
    1-85242-336-6

Haruko/Love Poems
    June Jordan
    1-85242-323-4

Stripping
    Pagan Kennedy
    1-85242-322-6

Spinsters
    Pagan Kennedy
    1-85242-405-2

The Medicine Burns
    Adam Klein
    1-85242-403-6

House Rules
    Heather Lewis
    1-85242-413-3

Bombay Talkie
    Ameena Meer
    1-85242-325-0

Armed Response
    Ann Rower
    1-85242-415-X

Nearly Roadkill
    Caitlin Sullivan and Kate Bomstein
    1-85242-418-4

Haunted Houses
    Lynne Tillman
    1-85242-400-1

Answer Song
    David Trinidad
    1-85242-329-3

Bedside Manners
    Luisa Valenzuela
    1-85242-313-7

The Roaches Have No King
    Daniel Weiss
    1-85242-326-9

Dear Dead Person and Other Stories
    Benjamin Weissman
    1-85242-330-7